BAMSES ÄVENTYR

BAMSE

SPÖKBORGEN

En dag spelar Bamse och Lille Skutt tennis.

– Slå inte så hårt, klagar Lille Skutt.

– Jag kan inte hjälpa att jag är världens starkaste björn, svarar Bamse.

Då kommer familjen Grävling förbi. De bär på alla sina saker.

– Hej! Ska ni flytta? ropar Bamse.

– Ja, suckar Herr Grävling. Vi vågar inte bo kvar bredvid den gamla borgruinen.

– Varför inte? undrar Bamse. Ni bor väl bra där?

– Nä, fy! Lillasyster Grävling skakar på huvudet. Det har börjat SPÖKA där.

– Ibland ylar det hemskt där inne. Fru Grävling pekar mot borgen.

– Säkert ett gammalt spöke som har vaknat, säger Herr Grävling.

Bamse tittar på familjen med bekymrad min.

– Vart ska ni ta vägen nu då?

Men det vet de inte.

Det tycker Bamse är förfärligt.

– Inte måste ni flytta. Jag går till borgen och tar en titt på spöket.

– Nä, gå inte! Lille Skutt hoppar upp och ner framför Bamse. Din styrka kanske inte hjälper mot spöken.

– Då får jag försöka prata vackert med det, säger Bamse och börjar gå mot borgen. Skalman och Katten Janson följer efter.

– Följer du också med, Lille Skutt? undrar Skalman.

– Bara en liten bit, säger Lille Skutt och hänger med öronen. Att träffa på ett spöke är det sista en liten rädd kanin vill göra.

Plötsligt hör de ett hemskt ylande från borgen.

Lille Skutt och Katten Janson blir så rädda att de hoppar in i buskarna. Skalman kryper in i sitt skal. Men Bamse går vidare.

– Det skulle jag aldrig våga, tänker Lille Skutt när kan kikar fram mellan bladen.

När Bamse kommer fram till borgen, upptäcker han att porten är låst.

– Synd att slå sönder en så fin port, tänker Bamse. Jag får klättra in genom ett fönster i stället.

Han hittar en glugg som står öppen och hoppar in.

– Ho, ho! Spöket! Var är du? hojtar Bamse. Men han får inget svar.

– Jag får väl leta upp det då. Jag börjar nere i källaren.

Då slår källardörren igen med en smäll.

– Konstigt! tänker Bamse. Var det någon som stängde den?

Det blir alldeles mörkt och Bamse ser ingenting.

– Jag har visst en ljusstump och tändstickor i fickan, säger Bamse. Vilken tur!

Nu kan han lysa upp den mörka trappan och fortsätta ner i källaren.

Plötsligt känner Bamse en hand på sin axel. Han vänder sig snabbt om.

– Vill du slåss? Jag varnar dej. Jag är världens starkaste björn.

Bamse tar tag i riddaren och kastar honom upp i luften. Han landar med ett brak på golvet.

– Hoppsan! Han rör sej inte, säger Bamse och går fram till honom.

– Stackars plåtgubbe! Hur gick det?

Förlåt om jag tog i för hårt. Bamse kikar in i rustningen.

– Den är tom! Det var märkligt.

– OOOOOYYYYL. Nu ylar det igen alldeles bakom Bamse. Han lämnar plåtgubben på golvet och går fram till gluggen.

– Spöket? Är du där?

Bamse lyser in i det mörka rummet och får syn på en dörr.

– OOOYYYLL, hörs det bakom dörren.

– Öppna eller jag slår in dörren, säger Bamse. Men ingen öppnar.

Utanför sitter Lille Skutt, Skalman och Katten Janson och väntar.

– Stackars Bamse! suckar Lille Skutt. Hur ska det gå för honom?

– Hejsan, grabbar! Bamse överraskar både Skalman, Lille Skutt och Katten Janson.

– Här kommer jag med det farliga spöket.

– DET!? Det är ju inget spöke, säger Lille Skutt. Det är bara en liten hund.

– Just det! säger Bamse. Han har väl gått och nosat i borgen och inte hittat ut. Då började han att yla.

– Typiskt spöken! ler Skalman. De är alltid något annat än man tror.

– Nu går vi och berättar för familjen Grävling att de kan flytta hem igen, skrattar Bamse.

BAMSE

LILLE SKUTT BLIR BORTRÖVAD

Idag tänker Bamse hälsa på Lille Skutt. Men på stubbens dörr hittar han ett brev. ”Till Bamse” står det skrivet med stora bokstäver.

– Vad kan Lille Skutt ha skrivit till mej? undrar han.

Men när Bamse läser brevet ser han att det inte alls är från Lille Skutt.

– Ruskige Rudolf!
Det förstår man väl vem som hittar på sånt, tänker han.

Bamse går med bestämda steg genom skogen och fram till Vargens kula. Han bankar hårt på dörren. Vargen ser förvånad ut när han öppnar och undrar vad som står på.

– Var gömmer du Lille Skutt, Ruskige Rudolf? dundrar Bamse.

– Jag gömmer ingen, säger Vargen.
Och vem är Ruskige Rudolf?

– Försök inte lura mej, säger Bamse. Jag ska låsa in dej hemma i garderoben, tills du erkänner. Han tar tag i Vargens svans och släpar honom efter sig.

På vägen träffar de Skalman. När Bamse visar honom brevet, plockar Skalman fram en skripto-transvideo-reservator ur skalet.

– En Skripto-vaddå? undrar Bamse.

– Med den kan man se vem som skrivit brevet, förklarar Skalman.

Och mycket riktigt. Efter bara en liten stund kommer det ut en bild ur apparaten.

– Men det är ju inte Vargen, säger Bamse förvånat när han tittar på bilden.

– Vem är det då? frågar Skalman.

– Vet inte. Ruskige Rudolf hade mask för ansiktet när han skrev brevet, svarar Bamse och släpper taget om Vargen.

Nu är Bamse mycket bekymrad. Han går hem och tömmer sin spargris. Men där finns bara nittiofyra kronor. Ruskige Rudolf vill ha hundra kronor.

– Har du sex kronor, Skalman?

– Javisst. Jag har dem någonstans här i skalet.

Vid midnatt smyger Bamse iväg till den ihåliga eken. Han lägger pengarna i trädet och sätter sig på vakt bakom en sten.

– Så kan jag se vem som hämtar pengarna, tänker Bamse.

Men ingen kommer.
När det blir morgon går han fram till eken och kikar in i hålet. Pengarna är BORTA!
Hur har det här gått till?
Plötsligt hör Bamse Lille Skutt ropa inifrån eken.

– Han måste vara inne i trädet, tänker Bamse och klättrar in genom hålet. Där hittar han en brant trappa som leder längre och längre ner i underjorden.

– Bamse! HJÄLP!
Nu hör han Lille Skutts röst igen. Bamse rusar nerför trappan.

Men det är inte Lille Skutt som Bamse hittar vid trappans slut. Det är bara en grammofon som spelar en skiva med Lille Skutts röst.

– Det sitter ett brev på den också. Nu är jag trött på de här dumheterna. Bamse går med arga steg fram till grammofonen.

Plötsligt trampar Bamse rakt igenom golvet och försvinner ner i ett djupt hål. Han landar med ett brak bland jord och tjocka trädrötter.

– Jag har inte en chans att klättra upp härifrån. Vem ska nu rädda Lille Skutt, suckar Bamse och kör uppgivet händerna i byxfickorna.

Då känner han något i fickan.
– En ask med dunder-honung!
Det är inte mycket, men tillräckligt för att Bamse ska orka slänga iväg den stora eken. När trädet är borta får Bamse syn på en ny trappa.
– Jag borde nog inte gå här. Men jag måste hjälpa Lille Skutt, tänker Bamse.

Han kryper genom smala gångar och springer upp och ner för branta trappor. Plötsligt stannar Bamse vid en stängd dörr.
– Vad är detta? Bamse plockar upp en ansiktsmask från marken. Den ser precis ut som Ruskige Rudolf på Skalmans bild.
Bamse knuffar upp dörren och …

…kommer rakt upp i Vargens kula.

– Just vad jag trodde! säger Bamse. Samme gamle bov som vanligt. Släpp genast loss Lille Skutt och ge tillbaka mina pengar.

Vargen blir så rädd för Bamse att han flyr in i spisen och upp genom skorstenen.

– Du vet att det inte lönar sig att göra rackartyg, Vargen. Nu får du gräva en ny gång istället, ropar Bamse när han och Lille Skutt traskar hemåt.

Ja, det hade Vargen inte tänkt på. Nu är den gamla gången inte hemlig längre.
– Kackerlackor och giftormar! muttrar Vargen för sig själv när han börjar gräva.
– Jag kommer inte hinna med några roligheter på flera månader. Grrr!

BAMSE

VARGEN OCH DUNDERHONUNGEN

Vargen är på väg till Bamses Farmor på Höga Berget.

– Farmors dunder-honung är dum, tycker han. Den gör bara Bamse stark. Alla andra får ont i magen i tre dagar.

– Undrar om hon har recept på dunder-honung för en varg? tänker han.

Vargen smyger fram till Farmors kök och kikar in.

– Vilken tur! Gumman ska ut och handla. Då ska jag snoka rätt på hennes kokbok. Vargen hittar den på köksbordet.

– Nu ska vi se. Kakor, bullar, soppor. Blää!! Bara vanlig gammal mat. Vargen bläddrar irriterat vidare.

– Men vad är det här? ”Motmedel mot dunder-honung”, läser Vargen. ”Om man häller i några droppar av detta medel förlorar dunder-honungen sin styrka.”

– UNDERBART! tänker Vargen.

Hos Farmor bor också Katten Janson och Husmusen. De kikar nyfiket fram bakom ett hörn.

– Vad gör Vargen här? undrar Katten Janson.

– Han skriver av något ur en av Farmors böcker, säger Husmusen.

– Konstigt! Vad ska han med det till? Katten Janson kliar sig fundersamt på nosen.

– Det måste vi ta reda på. Husmusen kilar snabbt in bland askan i spisen.

– Vad gör du? viskar Katten Janson.

– Vänta ska du få se. Husmusen springer upp på bordet och rakt över Farmors kokbok.

– Schas, musracka! väser Vargen. Han smäller igen boken och ger sig iväg.

– Nu ska vi se vad han skrev av, ropar Husmusen. Men varken Katten Janson eller Husmusen kan läsa. De måste be Farbror Gnag om hjälp. Han hittar sidan direkt, tack vare Husmusens smutsiga tassar som lämnat spår av aska i boken.

– Illa, illa! säger han. Det här är inte bra.

– Om Vargen smusslar ner sånt här i dunder-honungen, blir Bamse inte stark. Farbror Gnag fortsätter att läsa.

– ”VARNING! Om man tar tjugo skedar peppar istället för två, får man ett medel som gör dunder-honungen tio gånger starkare.” Husmusen funderar och räknar.

– Vi måste smuggla ner arton skedar peppar i Vargens motmedel. Då blir Bamse fortfarande stark av honungen.

– Bäst att sätta fart, säger Katten Janson och skyndar sig till Vargen.

Tysta smyger de in i Vargens kula. På golvet ligger alla ingredienserna till motmedlet. Katten Janson sniffar runt och letar efter pepparn. Men det skulle han inte gjort.

– AATSCHI! nyser han.

– Vad gör du här? Spionerar du på mej? Vargen fångar snabbt upp Katten Janson i svansen.

– Tro inte du kan stoppa mej, säger han och binder katten. Vargen fortsätter att röra ihop motmedlet.

– Jag klarar aldrig att hälla i pepparn ensam, suckar Husmusen från sitt gömställe.

Så snart Vargen är klar rusar han iväg till Höga Berget igen. Där står Farmor och lagar dunder-honung.

– Sådär ja! Nu är det färdigkokat.

När Farmor går till källaren efter burkar, smiter Vargen in och häller motmedlet i honungen.

Sedan gömmer sig Vargen utanför Farmors hus och väntar och väntar. Till slut kommer Bamse och hämtar sina honungsburkar.

– Ha! Nu är han snart inte världens starkaste björn längre, tänker Vargen illmarigt. Det måste jag berätta för Knocke och Smocke.

Under tiden har Husmusen lyckats gnaga av repet kring Katten Janson.

– Vi måste varna Bamse, säger Katten Janson. De stoppar honom på vägen tillbaka till Farmor.

– Mjau! Mjau! Mjau! jamar Katten Janson och hoppar upp och ner framför Bamse.

– Lugna dej, Janson.

Jag kan ju tappa burkarna. Bamse förstår inte vad katten vill utan fortsätter hemåt.

Då möter han Knocke, Smocke och Vargen.

– Hej, Bamse! Nu ska vi råna Nöffe i leksaksaffären, hälsar de glatt.

– Som de skojar. Det skulle de aldrig våga när jag har så mycket dunder-honung, tänker Bamse.

– HJÄLP! Det är Nöffe som ropar.

– Vilka tokstollar! Jag får väl ladda mej med en burk dunder-honung. Bamse sväljer med stora klunkar.

– Den smakade lite konstigt. Men Farmor vet nog vad hon gör.

Bamse rusar fram till Knocke, Smocke och Vargen som lastar en kärra full med leksaker.

– Hör ni, sluta med de där dumheterna. Jag är dunder-laddad.

– Hörde ni?
Hindra oss om du kan, hånar Knocke.

Bamse blir jättearg.
– Jag räknar till tre, sen kastar jag upp dej i en grantopp. ETT …
… TVÅ …
… TRE …
Knocke far iväg ända till Farmor på Höga Berget.
– Du store tid! Jag bara petade till honom lite, säger Bamse förvånat.

Farmor blir också förvånad.
– Hörru, kom du hit med raket? frågar hon när hon hittar Knocke utanför dörren.
– Nä, det var Bamse, piper Knocke ynkligt.
– Konstigt! Jag måste smaka på dunderhonungen, säger hon och letar upp Bamse och burkarna.
– Peppar-dunder! smackar Farmor. Jag måste genast göra ny. Du behöver inte vara tio gånger starkare än dej själv, lille Bamse.

– Hur gick det här till, undrar Katten Janson.

– Jag hann inte berätta innan du rusade iväg. Husmusen förklarar hur han hittat en blyertspenna och ritat dit en nolla efter tvåan på receptet. Då la Vargen i tjugo skedar peppar istället för två.

– Hur visste du var du skulle skriva? Du kan ju inte läsa, frågar Katten Janson.

– Jag kan läsa siffror, säger Husmusen stolt.

– Det var fiffigt gjort, tycker Katten Janson.

Utanför Vargens kula står två arga figurer som vill veta varför han lurat dem.
– Öppna dörren, din långnosade olycka, ropar Smocke.
– Jag ska ge dej för motmedel, morrar Knocke.

– Oj, oj, oj! suckar Vargen olyckligt. Hur ska jag någonsin våga gå ut igen?
– Varför höll jag mej inte vän med Bamse? De där rackartygen bara flyger i mej.

BAMSE

SKATTKISTAN

Bamse, Lille Skutt och Skalman har åkt till havet för att bada. När Bamse rott ut en bit från land, kastar han i ankaret.
– Så att båten inte driver bort när vi badar, säger Bamse.
Snart simmar och leker alla tre i det sköna vattnet.

När Bamse ska dra upp ankaret igen, märker han att det sitter fast.
– Jag får visst ta i ordentligt, säger Bamse och gör ett kraftigt ryck i repet. Bamse tar i så mycket att hela båten slår runt och alla far i vattnet med ett plask.

– Jag simmar ner och lossar ankaret,säger Bamse. På havsbottnen får han syn på en skattkista.
Men utan dunder-honung orkar han varken rubba ankaret eller lyfta upp skattkistan.

Bamse simmar upp igen och berättar för Skalman och Lille Skutt vad han hittat.
– Om du väntar här ska jag och Skalman ro iland och hämta honung till dej, säger Lille Skutt. Bamse sätter sig på den upp och nedvända båten och väntar.
Det dröjer inte länge innan Vargen får nys om vad Bamse hittat.
– Jag kan dela skatten med sjörövarna.
De kan segla ut och hämta den med sitt skepp, tänker Vargen slugt. Men sjörövarna är inte intresserade.
– Inte om Bamse vaktar skatten, säger Kapten Buster.
– Inte för miljoner kronor, säger Rusken.
– Nä, inte ens om vi får hundra glassar, säger Stollen.

– Men Bamse är inte dunderladdad, säger Vargen. Då får de fyra sjörövarna äntligen fart på benen.

– Varför sa du inte det med detsamma? undrar Slusken. De hoppar genast ombord på sjörövarskeppet och seglar rakt ut till platsen där Bamse väntar. Rusken och Slusken drar snabbt upp skattkistan. Utan dunder-honung kan Bamse bara sitta och titta på.

– Där seglar de iväg med skatten, suckar han.

Sjörövarna är stolta över att ha snott en skatt rakt framför nosen på Bamse.

– Hurra! Vi är rika! Tjolihoo! ropar de glatt. Men när de öppnar kistan ser de att den är alldeles tom. Inte en enda guldpeng finns där.

– Det finns inte ens botten i den, dundrar Kapten Buster

Sjörövarna blir arga på Vargen för att han lurat dem.

– Såna klåpare kastar vi i plurret, säger de och slänger honom överbord.

– Hjälp! Jag drunknar! ropar Vargen förtvivlat.

Men det bryr sig sjörövarna inte om, utan vänder skeppet och seglar tillbaka mot land.

Under tiden har Lille Skutt och Skalman fått tag på en ny båt och hämtat dunder-honung.

– Skynda er! ropar Bamse. Vargen håller på att drunkna. Han tar en stor klunk honung ur burken som Lille Skutt räcker honom.

– Kom här! säger Bamse. Han drar upp Vargen i båten, fast han varit dum och berättat för sjörövarna om skatten.

Sedan dyker Bamse ner i vattnet igen.

– Jag hoppas jag hittar ankaret, för det var rätt snyggt, tänker han. Då ser Bamse något som glimmar så fint på sjöbottnen.

– GULDPENGAR!

– Åh! tänker Bamse. Kistans botten sprack förstås när sjörövarna lyfte kistan. Pengarna blev kvar i havet utan att de märkte det. De tre vännerna delar skatten

i fyra lika stora delar. Bamse tycker nämligen att Vargen också ska ha en hög.

– Ska den elakingen ha? Nu är du för snäll, säger Lille Skutt.

– Elakingar behöver snällhet, svarar Bamse.

När Vargen går hem får sjörövarna syn på honom.
– Titta! Vargen har skatten, säger Rusken.
Den ska han inte få behålla, säger Kapten Buster och så rusar de efter honom.
– Hjälp! Sjörövarna låter mig inte vara ifred, så länge jag har pengarna, ropar Vargen till Bamse.

Bamse viskar något i Vargens öra och då vågar han gå hem igen.
Bråkar ni med Vargen ska jag kasta diskus med er, säger Bamse till sjörövarna.
– Usch! Bamse är värre än tandvärk och magknip på samma gång, muttrar Kapten Buster.

Men sjörövarna ger inte upp så lätt. De bestämmer sig för att gå till Vargen i alla fall. För säkerhets skull tar de med sig den stora skeppskanonen.

– Släpper han inte in oss, skjuter vi oss in, ryter Kapten Buster.

– Öppna! Annars skjuter vi dörren i småflisor, ropar Kapten Buster utanför Vargens kula.

– Jag har väl inget val, säger Vargen när han öppnar dörren.

– Hit med guldpengarna! Kapten Buster hotar med näven mot Vargen.

– Åh, nej!!!

Kapten Buster rusar ut igen.
– Har han en arg tiger som vakthund eller …? undrar Stollen förvånat.
– Nä, mycket värre! Bamse! ropar Kapten Buster.
– Usch, Bamse är en otäck, liten björn.
– Ja, han borde förbjudas. Sjörövarna springer därifrån så fort benen bär dem.

Men Vargen funderar en stund.

– Skönt att vara vän med Bamse. Hoppas att inte rackartygen flyger i mej igen, tänker han och ler när han ser hur sjörövarna försvinner iväg.

Australian Animals and their Young

Vincent Serventy

A family of young numbats (see page 18).
(Left) Mother and baby right whales (see page 32).

CHILD & ASSOCIATES
AN ALL-AUSTRALIAN PUBLISHER

Vincent Serventy, AM, Order of the Golden Ark, BSc, BEd, is president of the Wild Life Preservation Society of Australia. He has been writing books on Australian conservation themes for over twenty years. Among many others he has written such books as *Australia: A Continent in Danger*, *Australia's Natural Wonders* and *Dryandra*. He was Editor-in-Chief of the highly successful part-work *Australia's Wildlife Heritage* in the 1970s. He has participated in lecture tours throughout the United States and is well known internationally.

Brown booby chick begging food from an adult (see page 46).
Front cover: *Common wombat and her young* (see page 20).
Back cover: *White-naped honeyeaters and their chicks* (see page 61).
Endpapers: *Tasmanian devils* (see page 16).

Published by Child & Associates Publishing Pty Ltd,
5 Skyline Place, Frenchs Forest, NSW, Australia, 2086
A wholly owned Australian publishing company
This book has been edited, typeset and designed
in Australia by the Publisher
First edition 1988
Text by Vincent Serventy

Printed in Singapore by Kyodo-Shing Loong Printing
Industries (Pte Ltd)
Typesetting processed by Deblaere Typesetting Pty Ltd

National Library of Australia
Cataloguing-in-Publication Data

Serventy, Vincent, 1925–
Australian animals and their young.

Includes index.
ISBN 0 86777 293 X

1. Zoology—Australia. 2. Animals—Infancy.
I. Title.

591.994

All photographs not otherwise credited are by Vincent Serventy.

Contents

Introduction

What is a child?

Why does a child have an almost universal appeal? Most people automatically smile at human babies and at young animals of many kinds, especially rabbits, puppies and kittens. Is there some common factor? Konrad Lorenz, an authority in the field of animal behaviour, was the first to describe what he called 'releasers', that is sight, sound or smell patterns that trigger a particular kind of response; in the case of babies, the response is an affectionate, caring one.

Nikolaas Tinbergen continued the work of Lorenz and listed the factors that bring about parental feeling: short faces, large or at least prominent forehead, large round eyes, plump cheeks, and of course a positive reaction to an adult presence.

A well-worn teddy bear, a treasured possession of many a child.

A young koala, one of the most appealing of animals. (Photograph John S. Brownlie)

Disney Cartoons

'Baby faces' have been used by cartoonists all over the world. The Walt Disney favourites follow the pattern itemised by Tinbergen, and babyish features such as the large head, large eyes, and small nose are well developed. Stephen Jay Gould, an American scientist, studied Walt Disney characters over a number of years and found that the artists had steadily increased the 'baby' look. Eye size compared to the head increased from 27 to 42 per cent, and head length increased from 43 to 48 per cent of body length—so as Mickey Mouse grows older, he looks younger!

Gum-nut Babies

May Gibbs' gum-nut babies possess chubby roundness to an extraordinary degree while the wicked banksia men have all the hairiness and small eyes of abnormally developed adults. Toymakers have long been aware of the appeal of the 'supernormal' baby face. The very popular teddy bear is a good example. The chubbiness of bears in the United States led to the development of the toy teddy, while in Australia the baby-faced koala proved to be a successful variation of the teddy bear—despite the fact that in real life the adult koala can be a tough and bad-tempered animal.

Babies' behaviour is an added factor in the response they evoke. A very young human will smile at a complete stranger. A simple model of a head with two dark spots for eyes, or even a mophead, will produce a smile from a baby. In the animal world young mammals and birds may also show little fear of other animals at first, although the parents rapidly teach them to distinguish between friend and enemy.

Snugglepot and Cuddlepie are magnificent examples of the qualities that make young creatures attractive. These large-eyed, chubby gum-nut babies have delighted generations of children since their creation by May Gibbs.

3500 Million Years of Evolution

A highly developed relationship between parent and child is a fairly recent event in evolutionary history. When life began some 3500 million years ago, the first simple organisms were able to increase by each individual splitting into two. The new ones would split in their turn and, given good conditions, the few soon became billions.

Such simple life forms are so tiny that few of us are aware of the huge swarms that surround us in the water, in the soil, and in the air. Yeast is a good example of how rapidly such specks of life can multiply. In a kilogram of yeast there are some 11 million, million individuals. In twenty-four hours, given perfect conditions of food and space, these could divide into three tonnes of living material, or 33 thousand million, million individuals!

A variation of this simple division is the ability of an individual to send out bits of itself, for example seeds or spores, to spread its kind over a wider area. Launching tiny fragments of living material means that with luck the 'children' might grow well away from the parent. A mushroom can produce 16 thousand million spores, each of which is theoretically capable of becoming a new mushroom; fortunately for the other life on earth almost all fail to find a suitable, moist, warm spot.

Other individuals reproduce themselves by continuing to grow and budding off pieces of themselves. A young coral polyp might leave the parent or stay attached and so increase the size of the colony. Bracken ferns in an area may belong to one giant individual. If traced underground, they will be found to grow from creeping stems that send up shoots. Some wattles and sheoaks, and the strange and beautiful Christmas tree of south-western Australia, follow this pattern and a grove of these trees are all part of the original parent.

These are all successful methods of survival yet nature developed a new technique —creating two sexes so that two individuals could create a 'child' that shared the characteristics of both parents instead of only one.

In the early stages of more complex life forms, nature is still lavish with new individuals; eggs of sea hares are laid in strings of as many as 150 million. Almost all of these eggs are eaten by some other creatures, or the ocean would be packed with sea hares!

The Sydney rock oyster, too, pours out millions of eggs; the sea mullet can produce as many as two million. If all their young survived, five mullet could produce all the fish caught commercially in a year.

Yet even in fish some species produce fewer eggs and take greater care of them. Some carry them in their mouths until they hatch. Others, like the sea horses, carry them in a pouch, while some, like the gambusia or mosquito fish, produce the young inside the mother's body. The offspring come into the watery world alive and swimming, able to care for themselves.

In some insects, like the ants, bees and termites, the young remain with the mother to form huge colonies, while at the top of the evolutionary tree where care of the

Parent sooty tern and chick. The difference between the long-beaked adult and the shorter bill of the youngster is another example of the 'baby' look.

young is vitally important to success, we have the birds and mammals.

With birds, the time from mating to the production of young able to care for themselves may be a matter of months or much longer. Budgerigars can breed within four months of leaving the nest, but the magnificent wandering albatross has a breeding cycle of eleven months and a pair can nest only every two years. The young do not breed until they are about nine years old.

Mammals often give their children intense and long care. Sperm whales have a much longer gestation period than most other mammals—sixteen months from conception to birth. The baby takes milk from the mother for a year and, like the wandering albatross, does not breed until it is nine years old.

In the care of the young, humans are at the peak of the animal kingdom. The gestation period of nine months is followed by an intensive period of care and training, often lasting for years.

However, a number of animals, and even more plants, do very well without a father. Virgin birth or parthenogenesis is well known for many invertebrates, crustaceans and insects. Aphids can produce numerous young when conditions are good, but male forms appear when there is a need for eggs that can survive bad times. The complex life of a beehive is an example of the production of fertile and infertile offspring. It came as a shock to many naturalists when it was found in the last few decades that at least fourteen kinds of reptile produce young without the need for males.

Thus the patterns nature shows in caring for the young are almost endless. In some the father has been almost eliminated, in others males share, or in exceptional cases take the lion's share, in looking after the offspring.

Today we also have cloning, a process by which it is possible to create a plant or animal exactly the same as the original by using a nucleus from a cell of the parent. The age-old method of growing new, individual plants from a cutting is an example of cloning. Modern techniques have allowed scientists to develop the cloning of simpler animals such as amphibians and even of a mammal. The first case of a mammal being cloned was a house mouse. The nucleus from a mouse embryo was used in a female egg from which the original nucleus was removed. The egg was replaced in the mother and development followed, producing an exact copy of the first mouse. Even here the mother–child relationship remained as the baby was reared by the 'foster' parent.

The Future

Who knows what the future holds? In *Brave New World* Aldous Huxley foreshadowed cloning and hinted at the gradual replacement of family life with its cultural conditioning as we know it, for a factory production line where conditioning could be much more exact. So, perhaps we are lucky to live in a world where the unexpected can still happen and a child may grow up either like his parents or, sometimes excitingly, very different!

Dolls showing the childish features of short noses, big eyes and chubbiness, that adults find so appealing.

MAMMALS

In Australia we have examples of all three of the methods used by mammals to produce young. Most unusual are the egg-laying mammals that develop an egg in the mother's body; the platypus lays it in a suitable nest and the echidna carries it in a pouch. The newly hatched young, however, are fed on milk from the mother's body, the characteristic of all mammals.

In all other mammals the embryo is nourished for a time in the reproductive system of the mother. In the marsupials this time is short and although in some cases a placenta may be developed, it does not nourish the youngster for long.

In the placental mammals, a mass of tissues and blood systems forms in the wall of the uterus and the embryo is nourished there for many days. Some mammals have a short stay in the mother's body, some an extraordinarily long one. The northern brown bandicoot has the shortest gestation period, between 12 days 8 hours and 12 days 11 hours; the elephant has the longest, between 607 and 641 days. Some placental mammals such as house mice have a gestation of about twenty days, close to that of marsupials, and the young mice are born blind and relatively helpless.

After the marsupial baby has been born and made the perilous journey to the pouch to fasten on the nipples, it makes up for the short time inside the mother by a very long stay in the pouch. The grey kangaroo joey lives for about 300 days in the pouch and keeps on suckling until it is eighteen months old.

Antechinus

An interesting behaviour pattern in marsupial mammals is shown by the antechinus. By the time the youngsters are born all the adult males have died, worn out by sexual activity! Most of the mothers die soon after the young are weaned in spring, and only one in five survive to produce another litter in the next year.

These are only a few of the remarkable mother and child patterns found in egg-laying, marsupial, and placental mammals around the world. *(Photograph National Photographic Index, A. G. Wells)*

Echidna *(Left and right)*

Just before egg laying, the mother echidna develops a skin pouch and with considerable agility inserts the egg into this snug shelter. The egg hatches after ten days and the baby is fed on milk for about fifty days. The spines of the baby begin to grow just before it leaves the pouch, making it an uncomfortable burden for the parent. 'Worse than breadcrumbs in the bed', said one naturalist when describing how the mother might feel having such a prickly bundle in her skin pouch! When it has grown as large as the one in the photo *(right)*, it is placed in a burrow or some other shelter.

Platypus *(Below and overleaf)*

The most remarkable of the Australian mammals is this strange creature that has a bill like a duck, a tail like a beaver, webbed feet and a fur-covered body. And as if that is not eccentric enough, the mother lays eggs and feeds her young on milk.

Both male and female live in short burrows but when breeding approaches, the female digs another burrow that may be from 5 to 30 metres long. At the end of it she makes a nest of wet leaves and grass and builds plugs to block the tunnel from the outside world. She lays one to three eggs here, which are slightly moist and stick together. The tiny eggs are about 10 millimetres in diameter.

The mother then curls her body around this precious bundle until the babies, about 25 millimetres long, hatch ten to twelve days later. They suck milk from pores on the mother's abdomen and during this time she devours enormous quantities of food, sometimes eating almost her own weight in a single day. The babies are blind for the first eleven weeks, but are ready to explore the outside world at the age of four months.

Platypus are very difficult to observe and much of our knowledge comes from the devoted work of naturalist David Fleay, who is the only person to have bred the animal in captivity. *(Photograph page 13 The Australian News and Information Bureau; photograph left National Photographic Index, H. D. Miller)*

Western Quoll

In earlier times most Australian animals were called by names that were links with the more familiar creatures of Europe. We had kangaroo rats, anteaters, marsupial moles, native cats and the like. Today we call them by more suitable names, often those used by the Aborigines. Native cat has been dropped in favour of the Aboriginal word quoll. Australia has four species of quoll: the tiger, eastern, western and northern.

These baby western quolls, like all marsupials, are born as tiny scraps of naked flesh. For about seven weeks they cling to the mother's nipples. After about four months they leave the pouch or the mother's fur to shelter in a suitable place.

They spend this time in play; it is a period when they learn the skills they will need as adult hunters of live food such as small mammals, birds, reptiles and insects, although dead animals are also relished. *(Photograph National Photographic Index, A. G. Wells)*

Tasmanian Devil

During the last few years this fearsome-looking marsupial from Tasmania has become famous as a Disney cartoon character.

The early settlers, seeing an animal about the size of a small dog, that had black bristling fur and opened a wide pink mouth armed with powerful teeth when cornered, decided it was 'a very devil' of an animal.To its frightful appearance it adds a battery of bloodcurdling calls, but in reality these devils are harmless where humans are concerned.

When ready to breed the mother builds a comfortable nest deep in a hollow log or cave. Four is the usual family and they feed on milk in the mother's backward opening pouch until they are large enough to be left in the nest while she goes out to feed. Later they travel with her on these expeditions, either holding her fur or following at heel.

The Tasmanian devil is the largest of our carnivorous marsupials, but in the days when the Tasmanian tiger still existed, the devils played the role of the scavenger, following the larger tigers and eating the remains of any kill. The jaws are powerful enough to crush the strongest bones, such as the skull of a sheep. Today the devil is common in Tasmania, in the bush and scavenging around camps, and even on the outskirts of towns. *(Photograph Dave Watts)*

Common Dunnart

This tiny marsupial, looking like a small, plump kangaroo, is found across southern Australia with one population living in north Queensland. Drivers may see them caught in the car headlights on lonely country roads.

It is a marsupial flesh-eater, hunting small creatures such as insects and spiders, but naturalists wanting to trap them usually use a bit of peanut butter and oatmeal. A friend of mine, having found a family in a nest of dried grass in a hollow log, managed to rear and breed them. His pets lived on a diet of steak with extra insect titbits including cockroaches.

The dunnarts thrived, except for an occasional death caused by a domestic cat. Attracted by their odour the cats stole into the house at night and frightened the dunnarts by scratching at the wire of their cage in an endeavour to catch the morsels.

Litters of up to ten, as shown in the photograph *(left)*, can result in population explosions when conditions are good. *(Photograph R. Whitford)*

Planigale

The common belief that Australia is a land of gentle animals is a myth. In any region where there are plant-eaters, there will also be flesh-eaters. In Australia there are few large hunters, but in the world of the small, there are creatures as ferocious as any tiger.

The carnivorous marsupials called planigales are tenacious hunters, but their victims are grasshoppers and other insects. They measure only 13 centimetres from head to tail.

Planigales are not only animals of the bush. Some live in the heart of cities but they are usually revealed only if they are killed by domestic cats and brought into the house and displayed. Litters are large, up to a dozen, and as the animals grow they overflow from the pouch. When this happens they cluster in a sheltered spot such as a crack in the soil. *(Photograph National Photographic Index, R. Whitford)*

Numbat

The numbat is the most beautiful of all marsupials and since it feeds by day it is easier to see than most other native mammals, which tend to hide during daylight.

The major food is termites. The numbat scratches these insects out of their tunnels below the leaf litter, and also attacks them in their home galleries. The long pink tongue, which is about half as long as the body, lashes out through the corridors of the insect city and literally lassoes the termites.

The four babies do not crawl into a pouch after birth but settle on the teats at a patch on the underbody. Long hairs there keep the naked youngsters warm. Later, when they have grown a little, the mother digs a burrow that may be as long as 2 metres where they are kept warm in a snug nest of grass and leaves while they wait her return to feed them on milk. Sometimes these nests are made in hollow logs.

Youngsters are usually born in January and by year's end have left the home territory to make their own way in life.

The photographs show a family of youngsters at the burrow entrance *(above)* and the naked babies on the teats *(right). (Family photograph R. Whitford)*

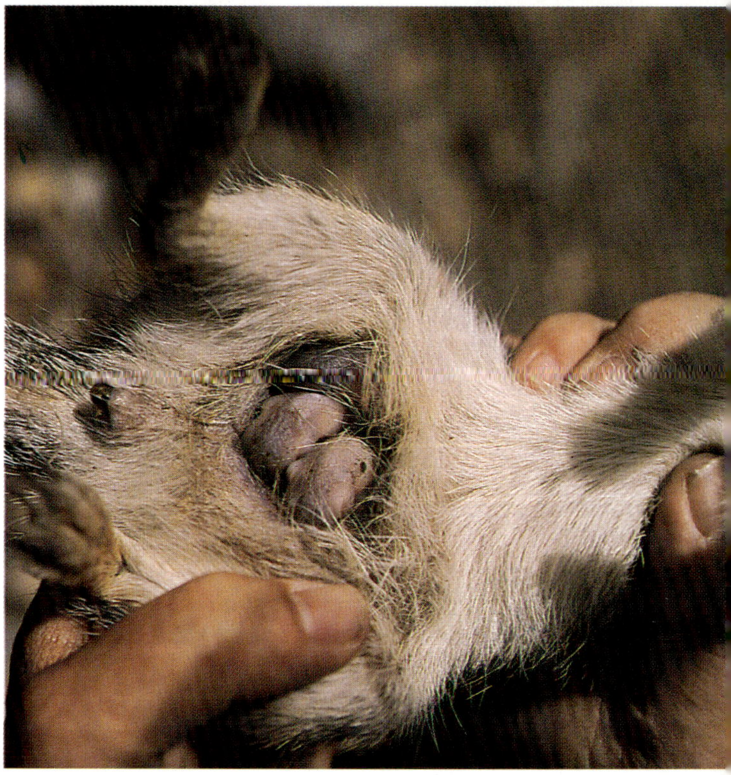

Bandicoot

Bandicoots are a much maligned group. They are as cheerful as any other native species in spite of the saying 'miserable as a bandicoot'. They forage through gardens like animated shovels, searching for insects and other small creatures. In the digging process young plants may be uprooted, but the bandicoots serve as gardeners' friends by destroying insect pests. They also dig out spiders and would devour wandering funnelwebs in Sydney gardens. Perhaps their disappearance from urban areas has led to an increase in funnelwebs!

There are nine kinds of bandicoots in Australia and all are long-nosed and able to smell prey in the soil. Each female has a backward-opening pouch. The reverse pouch is essential for a mother that digs for food because a pouch with its opening to the front would soon be filled with soil.

Bandicoots are rapid breeders and have the shortest gestation period of any mammal, some of only twelve and a half days. In some species the new baby weighs only 0.25 gram and is 13 millimetres long. The pouch often accommodates as many as eight and the teats are ranged in two rows of four.

At four months the young are able to breed, even though they are not fully grown. The males need only another month to become sexually mature so population explosions may take place when conditions are good. *(Photograph National Photographic Index, G. Rogerson)*

Common Wombat

This lumbering animal is regarded with affection by all Australians, except perhaps farmers whose rabbit-proof fences are undermined by its continuous burrowing. Wombats may dig tunnels up to 30 metres long, although they usually hollow out smaller ones, and shelter there from rain, wind, heat, fire, and other dangers.

Mating takes place in summer and the babies are born in typical marsupial fashion, climbing hand over hand from the birth canal to the backward-opening pouch guided probably by the smell of milk from the teats. If the blind, embryonic baby misses the target it will continue climbing along the mother's body and finally die.

The exact length of time spent in the pouch is not known but it ranges from seven to ten months. By the time the baby's weight increases from 1 gram to about 3 kilograms it is well furred and able to venture into the outside world. When it weighs about 14 kilograms it must look for a new burrow, helped on its way by the anger of the adult male who can weigh as much as 36 kilograms. *(Photograph Dave Watts)*

Koala

'A teddy bear come to life' is the best description of a koala, not only when it is a cuddly youngster but also when it is an adult. Even a surly, aggressive old male—a formidable fighter with a powerful grip and savage bite when molested—still keeps its appealing baby look.

The youngster starts life as a 2 centimetre scrap of flesh that climbs into the warmth and safety of the mother's pouch. It stays there for three months feeding on milk before taking a first look at the outside world. The pouch remains its home for another three months but it makes numerous trips to the mother's back when the weather is pleasant. Then comes the day when it leaves the pouch for good for a position on her back.

The mother weans the baby in a most unusual way, feeding it pellets of faecal material from her digestive tract.

Grey Kangaroo

'The wonderful kanguroo from Botany Bay' was the title of a London handbill urging passers-by to see this live marvel for only one shilling admittance. Not only was 'the shape, make and true symmetry of parts' remarkable, there was also the mystery of its birth.

Naturalists knew that it could not be born in the pouch but how did the blind, tiny baby manage that perilous journey? It has now been described many times. This is the birth pattern of the eastern grey kangaroo, but the same would hold for the western and other members of the kangaroo family, with modifications for other marsupials.

The female, often called the doe, sits on her tail which usually points forward. She prepares the pouch before birth so it is both moist and clean, holding it open with her front paws and pushing in her muzzle. A flow of fluid heralds the imminent arrival of the joey. It comes out head first and soon breaks from the birth membranes, aided partly by the mother's licking. If nothing disturbs the mother, the joey lines up with the pouch opening and climbs along, gripping the fur with its claws, and moving hand over hand until it reaches the teats inside.

This may take as little as fifteen seconds or as long as four minutes. Once inside, the joey fastens on to one of the four teats, which swells to hold it firmly in the pouch. Early settlers examining the pouch of a dead female would tug at the joey and because of the tight fit, the mouth would burst and bleed giving the impression that it actually grew from the teat like a coral polyp budding off from its parent! With gentle handling, however, the joey can be separated from the teat without damage.

The baby stays in the pouch for some eight months, then travels at foot until it is about a year old, when it still occasionally takes a drink from the parent.

Red Kangaroo

These giants of the inland plains raise their young in a way similar to the grey kangaroos. A persistent story about the kangaroos, first written by naturalist John Gilbert to his old employer John Gould, more than 100 years ago, is: 'If a female is pursued with a tolerably large young one in the pouch, she will often by a sudden jerk throw the little creature out, but whether this is done for her own protection, or for the purpose of misleading the dogs, has been debated by hunters, I am inclined to think the former, for I have observed the dogs pass on without noticing the young one, which in general crouches in a tuft of grass, or hides itself amongst the scrub without attempting to run, or make its escape. The mother, if she escapes, doubtless returns, and picks it up.'

It is true the young are often thrown out but it may be because the pouch may gape during high speed and if the doe makes a sudden turn, the baby is thrown out in the original direction by the momentum. It is doubtful if the mother returns to pick up the joey but at least it has some chance for life.

The term red kangaroo is sometimes misleading, for in fact only those in the western parts of Australia are red. In the east, the colours of the buck and the doe differ, with the male having a red body and blue-grey extremities, and the female being wholly blue.

Whiptail or Pretty-face Wallaby

Both these names are apt ones. The long tail, even longer than the total body length, is a feature of this marsupial, and it is particularly noticeable when the animal is on the move. Yet pretty-face is also deserved, for few sights in the Australian bush are more delightful than a joey peering out of a whiptail mother's pouch.

The babies, after a gestation of about thirty-six days, climb into the pouch where they are fed on milk for about nine months. They then leave this snug harbour but continue to suckle for another six months.

The pretty-face, which today ranges from the mid-New South Wales coastal forests northward as far as Cooktown, is unfortunately shot as a pest in some parts of Queensland. Native animals may become minor pests on farms developed in the middle of forest country but electric fencing has been found to be an effective way of protecting such crops, and it is hoped that the pretty-face will be allowed to live peacefully as one of the most attractive members of the Australian bush.

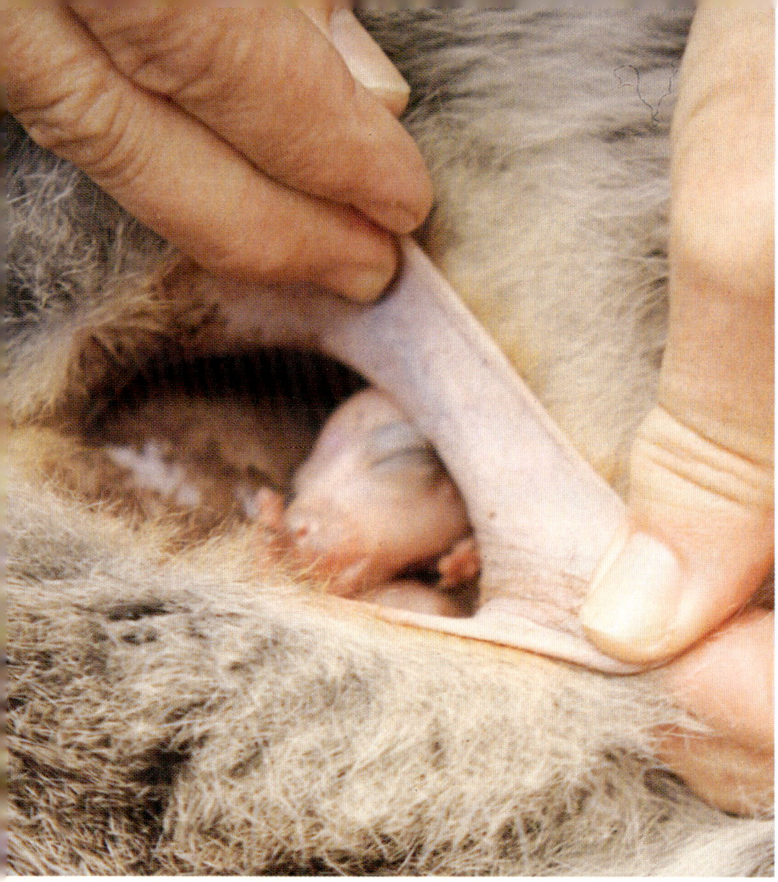

Tammar Wallaby

'... procreation is very miraculous, yea, worthy to note; under the belly the females have a pouch into which one can put a hand, and in that she has her nipples, where have discovered that in there their young grow with the nipple in mouth, and have found lying in it (the pouch) some which were only as large as a bean, but found the limbs of the small beast to be entirely in proportion, so that it is certain that they grow there at the nipple of the mammal and draw the food out of it until they are big and can run. Even though when they are very big they still creep into the pouch when chased and the mother runs off with them.'

So wrote Francis Pelsaert, the Dutchman whose ship the *Batavia* was wrecked on the Abrolhos Islands near Geraldton in 1629. His error in thinking the young are born in the pouch was a belief shared by many bushmen, although not by naturalists.

The tammar wallaby still lives on the islands where Pelsaert studied it, and also on islands south to Kangaroo Island in South Australia and on the nearby mainland.

Red-necked Wallaby

The red-necked wallaby can breed at any time of the year and after a gestation period of about thirty days the joey follows the same pattern as other members of the kangaroo family.

The young leave the pouch after six months and in some regions mothers may give birth every nine months. An adult can live at least seventeen years, so huge numbers may appear when conditions are good.

The red-necked wallaby is common along the east coast of Australia. In Tasmania it is often called the Bennett's wallaby or bush kangaroo.

Agile Wallaby *(Right)*

Many members of the family of kangaroos are solitary animals, going their way singly, and coming together only when ready to mate, or when drought reduces the food supply so that many must gather at the few good feeding places.

The agile wallaby of northern Australia is possibly one of the most solitary. A few males may gather around a female when she is receptive, but after a brief encounter she wanders away to bear her youngster. The baby has a seven-month pouch life and remains at foot for a very short period compared to other kangaroos. The female is able to mate when she is about 350 days old, so populations can build rapidly.

Quokka

The first Dutch explorers found Rottnest Island overrun with what seemed to be large rats, so they called the place Rottnest, the Dutch version of 'rat nest'. Later it was learned the females kept their young in a pouch, like so many Australian mammals. This marsupial is a kind of small wallaby, now known by its Aboriginal name of quokka.

Intense study of the quokka that lives only in south-western Australia revealed many of the secrets of marsupial physiology and birth.

Dingo *(Right)*

Few animals have aroused as much controversy as Australia's wild dog, the dingo. In a sense it is a feral animal since it was brought here by Aborigines some time during the last 10 000 years. It spread over the mainland but failed to reach Tasmania because of the barrier of Bass Strait.

The dingo is related to the domestic dog and is sometimes regarded as the same species. Indeed its life history is similar, except that the dingo has a breeding season which may begin in late autumn and continue through the winter.

After a gestation period of sixty-three days, the young are born in a suitable den—a rock cave or a hollow in the ground. With an average of five young the mother often needs help in feeding them.

The pack may consist of the male and female as well as young from the previous season, for although they can breed when nine months old, they rarely do. Mateship in dingoes is similar to that found in many Australian birds, where young from previous broods assist their mother. As well as helping the mother with the care of the cubs a pack can kill larger prey like an adult kangaroo, and so help to provide food for the litter.

One-humped Camel

The camel is one of the most efficient of all the animals that live in desert country. It can survive without water far longer than a horse or other large animals. It can carry a load impossible for a horse for a long distance and, when well treated, is easier to handle than a horse, according to those who run camel safaris in the Australian bush.

Camels usually travel in groups with an older female as the leader, except during the breeding season when a male moves in to take charge.

The baby takes about a year to develop in the mother's body and when born weighs about 40 kilograms. The youngster is at once able to move along with its mother and she feeds it on milk for about a year. A fully grown camel can reach a weight of about 700 kilograms, making it the largest land animal in Australia.

Brought to Australia more than one hundred years ago it is considered a pest in some areas.

Wild Horse

The white settlers brought domestic horses to Australia with them. A few escaped, thrived in the bush, and became the wild horses called brumbies. No one is sure of the reason for this name, although there was a pioneer horse breeder named James Brumby.

Domestic horses range in weight from about 140 kilograms for a Shetland pony to 1000 kilograms for a draft horse, and brumbies are about midway, around 400 to 500 kilograms.

Females carry the baby for about a year. A few hours after birth the foal can run along with the mother. It has long legs compared to its parent's but its body grows a little faster than the legs and catches up. A horse can live for about thirty years.

This mare and foal *(right)* are wild horses on Fraser Island, Queensland.

Water Buffalo

In 1825 the first water buffaloes were brought from Timor to Melville Island. Since then they have spread over the wetter sections of the Northern Territory and have become a destructive element in the local environment.

Recent work has shown that there are four castes—male, female, juvenile and calf. In the dry season males and females lead separate lives and herds of up to 500 cows may live together. With the coming of the wet the bulls return and the calves are born, then with the return of the dry, they separate once more. Female calves remain with their mothers, probably for life, while the young bulls leave after two or three years, departing from the female group because of the attacks of a dominant bull.

The family groups form clans and the arrival of the baby is an important event. When the cows leave their shelter to graze, an adult stays to guard the youngsters.

The mother licks the newborn baby and probably taste and smell are important in cementing the mother–child bond. When the young are threatened and utter distress calls, all the group, not only the mother, rally to defend all the young.

Feral Donkey *(Right)*

These beasts of burden played an important part in the settling of northern Australia, particularly in the more arid areas. Many were turned loose when motor transport replaced donkey teams and today the wild population may number up to 125 000 and is proving a problem in parts of Australia.

Like a pony with big ears, the donkey has long been associated with man since it was tamed from African wild asses. Its life history is very similar to that of the horse.

Right Whale

The most colossal mothers the world has ever known are the whalebone or baleen whales, those marine mammals that plough through the oceans of the world, sifting out myriads of crustaceans called krill. From this diet of small fry is created the bulk that makes them world giants.

Right whales were hunted relentlessly until by the 1850s they were almost extinct. In 100 years of protection there has been a small revival and every year a few mothers come to sheltered bays in Australia to give birth.

Gestation is long, sixteen months in the sperm whales and probably at least a year in the right whales, but growth is rapid. It has been estimated that a young blue whale feeding on its mother's rich milk doubles its weight in seven days. A human baby takes at least 120 to make that kind of increase.

The baby right whale is suckled for about a year so the female can give birth only every second year. *(Photograph D. Hembre)*

Australian Sea Lion

Sea lions are found in breeding colonies from Kangaroo Island westward to islands north of Perth. The male with his almost black fur and creamy mane deserves the name of lion. He is bulky, weighing up to 400 kilograms, and is a formidable fighter. The female is lighter at about 150 kilograms and is silvery-grey and cream. After its birth pelt of dark brown the baby moults into the mother's colouring.

The gestation period is a long one, probably eleven months, and the babies are born weighing up to 12 kilograms. Their weight rises rapidly and it seems as though they take milk from the mother until the next baby is born about eighteen months later. They supplement the milk when older with the normal seal diet of fish, squid and other molluscs.

Fortunately, with strict protection, the Australian sea lion population appears stable at up to 10 000 individuals, out of a total Australian seal population of about 50 000. This includes the fur seals, which are far more common.

Southern Elephant Seal

The giant southern elephant seals once bred on King Island in Bass Strait. All kinds of seals were hunted in the early days of settlement—for their skins and for the oil in their bodies—and the Australian elephant seals were destroyed.

A lone animal occasionally wanders north to Australia but they have not yet started a colony. A few mothers have given birth on the Tasmanian coast over the last thirty years, so there is a chance they might settle here once more. It may be possible to help nature a little by releasing some pups from colonies on Macquarie Island on a suitable island in Bass Strait, in much the same way as koalas were taken to islands off the Victorian coast, where they flourished.

Male elephant seals are huge and can weigh just under 4000 kilograms. The females are very much lighter, a big one weighing only 350 kilograms. A big male collects a harem of females and in the safety of his protection each mother gives birth to a baby that weighs about 30 kilograms. Feeding on the mother's rich milk, it increases to 150 kilograms in less than a month. Then the mother mates with the harem bull leader and goes back to the sea.

Dugong

'... they were not as beautiful as they are painted though they had something of a human face ...' wrote Christopher Columbus on 9 January 1493 when he saw his first manatees, the marine mammals whose relatives gave rise to the mermaid legend.

Perhaps the dugongs of the Red Sea were taken for mermaids when the babies were seen being fed from nipples on the sides of the chest next to the base of the flippers.

The Australian dugong is still reasonably common; the adults can be 3 metres long and about 400 kilograms.

Gestation appears to take about twelve months and babies have been recorded up to 1.75 metres long. The youngster stays with the mother for about a year, keeping close and usually swimming above her; perhaps her 'slipstream' helps it along. Sometimes the calf rides in piggyback fashion up to the surface.

In one case, when dolphins began to harass the mother and baby, other adult dugongs formed a screen around the calf to protect it. *(Photograph Ben Cropp)*

BIRDS

Animals with feathers

The change of a scale into a feather was a tremendous evolutionary development; birds took a giant step forward compared to reptiles, although exactly how these great leaps in evolution occur is a hotly disputed scientific argument.

Birds, having evolved from reptiles, share some of the characteristics of their far-off ancestors, including scales on the feet and egg laying. The fossil of the first-known bird, Archaeopteryx, could have been mistaken for a reptile with its teeth, solid bones and long tail, except that it also had feathers, the mark of the birds.

The body temperature of a reptile can rise higher than that of any mammal or bird. The ability to keep a stable temperature is well developed in both birds and mammals and is an important factor in their survival in Arctic and Antarctic regions. However some mammals and birds can lower their temperatures in reptilian fashion.

Birds and mammals are described as warm-blooded, and reptiles and all other creatures as cold-blooded. But the terms are misleading. It would be more accurate to say that some animals depend mainly on inner heat and some on outer heat. Surprisingly, some insects, large fish, and also a few reptiles, as well as the mammals and birds, are among those that depend on inner heat. Warm-blooded creatures must eat more to keep warm, but despite this they have dominated the natural world. One theory that explains the success of the dinosaurs over millions of years is that they were 'hot-blooded'.

Another factor in the birds' success, apart from being warm-blooded, may have been the increasing care of their young. With the hard-shelled egg came more parental care. Certain bird species show a reptilian pattern by laying eggs in sand warmed by volcanic vents, but in most other birds there is a long and close relationship between adults and young.

Eggs

Egg size can vary from the tiny 15 x 11 millimetres of the weebill to the 140 x 95 millimetres of the cassowary. The malleefowl lays an egg one-seventh of her own weight. There are two major groups of chicks: those like plovers or gulls that hatch fully feathered from eggs that are about 10 to 15 per cent of the mother's weight, and those that hatch naked and helpless, such as wagtails and wrens, and come from eggs that are only about 5 per cent of the weight of the mother.

Once a chick inside the egg has developed enough to be able to break into the tiny air pocket enclosed in the shell, and take a deep breath, it is then also able to take an intelligent interest in life both outside and inside the shell. By hearing its own calls a young duckling learns to recognise its relatives in the outside world, particularly its mother which it identifies by listening to her calls. Visual clues come after hatching, with the chick accepting as its mother any bird that sounds right. This is called 'imprinting'.

A peacock imprints on a kangaroo!

If a duckling peers out of a nesting hollow 30 metres above ground and the mother calls it from below, the baby will launch itself into space without fear. Being mostly feathers it will float down without harm.

Imprinting

There is fascinating information about the emergence of the chick from the egg. It has been known for centuries that some domestic birds, particularly hens and geese, will follow the first moving object they see on hatching. A duckling will follow a hen or a gosling, or even the goose girl.

Sometimes birds in captivity will become attached or imprinted to bizarre objects. One unfortunate budgerigar became imprinted to a ping-pong ball! A friend of mine, an accomplished bird mimic, decided to brighten the life of a female turkey raised alone on a farm by imitating a male turkey gobbling. The bird stared at him, puzzled, but finally walked to him and crouched in the mating position. Ever after, when my friend visited this farm, much to his embarrassment, the bird would rush up to him and crouch!

Southern Cassowary

The cassowary nests during winter and early spring and four eggs are the normal clutch. As with the emu, the male takes over and both incubates and rears the youngsters, which are attractively striped when they hatch.

Many bird species defend their eggs and young vigorously, with the cassowary being no exception. With a body weight of around 50 kilograms, this bird has been recorded as having killed people with blows from its powerful legs. This has happened in both Australia and Papua New Guinea.

Emu

The female emu is one of the few birds that leaves the rearing of her chicks entirely to her mate. After laying a clutch of about ten eggs, her duty is done. The male then takes over the work of incubating the eggs and looking after the chicks for 18 months. Indeed, at least in captivity, a liberated female may even lay several clutches for several husbands.

The father cannot leave the nest for two months while he is incubating the eggs, during which time he loses about 5 kilograms in weight. If an enemy approaches the nest, he will lay his neck along the ground so that he looks like a bush and will be undetected. A similar behaviour pattern in nesting ostriches led to the incorrect belief that they 'buried their heads in the sand'.

When the last chick breaks out of its egg the father leads his flock on a nomadic life that continues for a year and half. During this time the chicks change from prettily striped babies to brownish gawky youngsters before they develop the adult plumage.

Fairy or Little Penguin

Like many seabirds the parent penguins look alike and share in the nesting duties. The fairy penguin is Australia's only nesting penguin although others visit here. With an incubation period of about forty days and a nestling period of two months, it is obvious a great deal of food gathering and care are needed.

The chicks are born blind and helpless although they are covered with warm down. Another coat of down develops before the final moult into adult feathers. *(Photograph Dave Watts)*

Shy Albatross (White-capped albatross)

The shy albatross is Australia's one nesting albatross. The rookeries of these birds are found on the storm-swept islands off Tasmania—Albatross Rock in Bass Strait, and Pedra Branca and Mewstone off the Tasmanian coast.

Seabirds such as petrels and albatrosses have particular problems in raising young as they must range over enormous areas to gather food and then carry the catch inside the crop rather than in the beak like most other birds.

Most petrels nest in an underground burrow but the albatrosses live above ground. A chick makes a food-begging call as it probes towards the parent's head. The adult opens its beak and the chick pushes its own bill inside at right angles and above the tongue. The parent regurgitates the food and it passes into the chick's gullet.

As with all seabirds of these groups, the incubation is long, about two months, and it is another four and a half months before the shy albatross nestling takes its first flight.

Shearwater

The best-known species of shearwater is the short-tailed shearwater, or Tasmanian muttonbird, of southern Australia. Seabirds around the world have been used for food for thousands of years, and the Tasmanian muttonbird is still harvested on a number of islands in Bass Strait.

The adult shearwater lays her single egg at some time during a twelve-day period, from 19 to 21 November to 30 November to 2 December, on one of the nesting islands from east to west. This timetable has been unvarying since the first records were kept in the early days of white settlement.

The egg is laid in a burrow deep in the soil. Either the old burrow is cleared, or a new burrow is dug. Both parents share the incubation and later the feeding of the young. The fledglings are ready to leave between the third week in April and the first week in May. In this last stage of the life of the nestling they are harvested in a short season that begins on 27 March and ends on 30 April.

Although this industry is one of the oldest in Australia the numbers of short-tailed shearwaters are steadily rising and they are colonising islands as far north as Sydney and as far west as the Recherche Archipelago in Western Australia.

This shearwater is probably the best-known bird species in the world, having been intensively studied since 1949 because of its scientific as well as its commercial interest.

Least Frigatebird (Lesser Frigatebird)

These sea marauders get most of their fish and cuttles second-hand by pirating other seabirds, particularly boobies. A victim returning from a successful day's fishing will be buffeted until it disgorges part of its catch, which the frigatebird skillfully snaps up before it reaches the sea.

The photograph shows a chick shouting defiance at the photographer!

Red-tailed Tropicbird

The plumage of this beautiful seabird is almost entirely snowy while a rosy flush appears on the body early in the courting season. Two red streamers about half a metre long project from the tail and when the adults hover over their nesting sites, these often spread in a spectacular fashion. When winds are strong, tropicbirds can hover or even drift slowly backwards with the airstream.

Nests are usually placed in a protected place, often in an overhang forming a cave or under a bush. Usually only one egg is laid, directly on the sand, and the chick begins life covered in grey down. Gradually it sheds this and develops elegant feathers with black bars on the white. Later these moult and the adult plumage develops.

Nesting birds face enemies such as sea eagles but, although not common, tropicbirds appear to be increasing their range into the more southern parts of Australia.

Australian Pelican

Pelicans build their nests on the ground, sometimes on the bare earth, but usually a collection of sticks or other material is pulled into the site while the adult incubates the eggs.

The baby pelican is hatched naked and helpless. Some weeks later the youngster will grow a good covering of down and the beginning of wing feathers. The young birds often form creches while waiting for the return of their parents from the day's fishing.

The huge bill of the pelican is a food gathering device similar to that of the baleen whale. With beak wide open the bird scoops water and small fish then closes the bill and allows the water to escape at the corners of the mouth while the fish are trapped inside.

Pied Cormorant

Five kinds of cormorant, better known as shags, live on Australian freshwater and seashores. The pied cormorant, one of the two largest species, is found around the whole of the Australian coastline. In the eastern States it explores rivers and lakes in the outback. The birds in the photograph were nesting on an island in Lake Eyre. Tens of thousands of nesting pied cormorants found plentiful food in this 'inland sea' which has filled only twice since white settlement.

The nest is a substantial platform of sticks, often placed on a rock pinnacle. When food is plentiful clutches of five eggs are common. They hatch as naked and, to human eyes, ugly babies but soon grow a covering of down and, later, the adult feathers. As with the booby, the adult regurgitates its catch directly into the mouth of the chick. Mother and father share the nesting duties.

Cormorants are good swimmers and can pursue their prey under the water. Once caught the slippery victims are held tightly by the sharp edges of the bill and the hooked tip. The smaller species also eat yabbies, crabs and other water creatures.

Brown Booby

Tropical gannets nesting on islands in rarely visited seas were safe until people arrived. The first visiting sailors found the birds completely unafraid. Easily killed for fresh meat, they earned the name of booby—too silly to know humans were dangerous!

Today they are protected and the nesting birds are gradually losing their fear. Once again birds on the nest can be watched with ease.

The nests vary from almost bare ground to a platform of sticks and other material placed on the earth. Usually two eggs are laid. Both parents incubate them, sitting stolidly on the eggs, not to keep them warm but to shade them from the tropical sun. Both parents also care for the young. They regurgitate the food they have caught, passing it directly into the bill of the baby. In this photograph a chick is food-begging from an adult that has just returned to the nest.

Masked Booby

'Little birds in their nests agree', but not always! The masked booby female lays two eggs but the chick that hatches first has the advantage in pushing forward for food. It grows larger and stronger while the second becomes weaker until finally it dies.

The parents share in the nesting duties, incubating the eggs for about six weeks. The newly hatched baby often sits on the parent's feet, perhaps to avoid the heat of the tropical sand. An older chick will approach an adult with beak pointing upward and neck waving in supplication. This behaviour triggers the parent's response and the youngster is fed with food regurgitated by the adult. Four months pass before the young can take care of themselves and join the fishing groups.

Sooty Tern

A colony of sooty terns is an exhilarating sight, where hundreds of thousands of birds offer a bewildering variety of behaviour. Some are still setting up house, others sitting quietly on eggs or feeding insistent young. Immature birds stand in quiet groups waiting for returning parents, wondering if they should try their wings over the nearby ocean.

Incubation time for the sooty tern egg is twenty-six days and a few days after hatching the chick leaves the nest. This is a dangerous period for the immature tern as a straying youngster is often pecked by other breeding birds. The nests are only about a metre apart, so it must tread warily. A month later the chicks are feathered and they move into large creches along the beach.

Crested Tern

Crested terns are often mistaken for silver gulls as they are about the same size, but the bill is yellow. Also, instead of landing on the water and bobbing for food, they dive under the water to seize the fish. Indeed they are often called 'divers', to separate them from gulls.

They nest in noisy and often large colonies on islands in a scrape in the ground. Usually only one egg is laid, but sometimes when there is plenty of food there are two.

Like the chicks of gulls, crested tern babies crouch in the nest to avoid being seen. When slightly older they scurry into the shelter of bushes, often plunging their head into the plant and leaving their rear protruding. The youngster does not move so the camouflage saves it from detection.

Silver Gull

The silver gull, a scavenger of the beaches, is one of the best known of all Australian birds. It ranges well inland, however, even appearing around Alice Springs or in other desert places when occasional floods create ideal conditions for many kinds of waterbirds.

Silver gulls normally nest on islands, both natural and artificial. The nest is a fairly substantial structure of plant material and the female lays two or three eggs, although when food is plentiful the clutch may be as many as five. The gulls nest in colonies sometimes numbering as many as thousands, particularly when a large rubbish tip provides abundant food. In some areas they may nest twice a year, in both autumn and spring.

The chicks are beautifully camouflaged and when crouching on the ground or in a shrub are almost impossible to see. They grow to resemble their parents, but immature birds lack the red bill and legs of the adults.

Reef Heron (Eastern Reef Egret)

The elegant reef heron is a creature of offshore reefs where it catches small fish as well as other marine creatures. Two colour forms occur, one snow white and the other a slaty grey. White birds are normally more common in tropic regions, with the grey forms increasing in the cooler south.

Both forms may mate, and dark and light chicks can be found in the same brood. Occasionally a pied youngster appears.

The reef heron's nest is an untidy stick platform, typical of all the group. Usually built deep in the island trees, the nests can survive strong winds. From two to five eggs are laid and the number of young raised depends on the amount of food available to the parents.

White-faced Heron

The white-faced heron builds a nest of twigs high in trees even in suburban areas. The incubation period is from three and a half to four weeks and the nestlings stay at the nest for another month. It is the most common of the heron-like birds found around Australia and is often called the blue crane. *(Photograph W. R. Taylor)*

Black Duck

Black ducks nest in typical duck fashion in long grass or in shrubbery near or in water, or in a hollow in a tree. Ten is the normal clutch.

As with many species the ducklings' attractive markings help to camouflage them when they 'freeze' on a warning call from their parents. Camouflage is most effective when there is no movement and the ability to lie perfectly still is very important to the survival of the young of many animals.

This duck is more grey than black so the name is puzzling. It is the Australian equivalent of the European mallard, although the male never develops the bright breeding plumage of the northern species. Because mallards were brought to Australia and interbreeding is common, some offspring show hybrid features—orange feet and a purple-blue speculum, the bright patch of colour on the wing.

Maned Duck

The female maned duck lays about ten eggs in a nest usually in a hollow tree and the drake guards the site from other males. The mother encourages the newly hatched chicks to come to the ground by flying down then up to the nest several times, calling steadily.

When the ducklings have floated safely to earth the parents gather them in line and head for the nearest water, perhaps several kilometres away. Here the ducklings stay until they are able to fly, and then a number of family groups join to form a larger flock.

The maned duck is found over much of Australia where there are suitable areas for feeding and breeding.

Black Swan

Hans Christian Andersen's story *The Ugly Duckling* has brought comfort to children everywhere, no matter how inaccurate its natural history. Baby white swans are attractive creatures and the baby black swan is even more appealing, at least in the first few days of life; it does have a gawky stage before assuming the stance and plumage of the graceful adult bird.

Using grass and reeds, swans build floating island nests in shallow water. In larger colonies females may do all the work of raising the young, but in smaller lakes the parents share the duties. The bond between mother and father can be very strong, and the birds may mate for life. Sometimes the young from the first clutch help rear the second. This family assistance is remarkably common in Australian birds; mateship in practice!

Royal Spoonbill

This bird of the swamp lives up to its name of 'royal' during the breeding season. At this time, which may be from spring to early winter, both male and female grow beautiful nuptial plumes on the crown and nape that contrast vividly with the black bill.

The bulky stick nest is usually built in a tree above water, and the mother lays up to four eggs. Male and female share in incubation and in feeding the chicks. The strange spoonshaped bill develops as the chick grows.

The adults feed in shallow water, sweeping the head backward and forward with the bill slightly open, catching fish and crustaceans in its huge spread. When the food is safe inside the bill the bird flicks its head upward and the victim slides into its mouth.

Brolga

The stately brolga is a member of the crane family and like all this group is one of the most elegant of birds. The brolga also indulges in remarkable dancing displays both in and out of the breeding season. The displays probably strengthen the link between male and female. Sometimes a sudden noise, such as a car horn, will start a pair dancing.

Nesting is a simple matter of building a platform of plants, about 1.5 metres in diameter, on the ground, usually near water although farm dams have been accepted as suitable.

Two eggs are laid and once hatched the chicks move off with their parents in search of food. Because brolgas feed on a wide variety of food, ranging from swamp bulbs to insects, they can live in many types of habitat. *(Photograph National Photographic Index, I. R. McCann)*

Jabiru

Storks are ancient symbols of fertility, mythology crediting them with the bringing of babies as well as good luck. The jabiru is Australia's only stork and, unlike the white European stork, the jabiru's plumage is a mixture of black and white. The red legs and feet add brilliance.

The immature birds in this photograph, feeding on the edge of a Kakadu lagoon, lack the splendour of the adults, being muddy brown with black legs.

The parents usually build the very bulky nest high in a tree and share all the nesting duties. In feeding, they regurgitate in front of the chicks which then pick up the food. In the tropical regions where the birds are most common, the parents also bring water to the nestlings and regurgitate it into their bills. After about four months the youngsters leave the nest to forage for themselves.

Little Bittern

This young bittern was almost at the flying stage when it was photographed. Bitterns live among the reeds of freshwater swamps but because of their excellent camouflage they are rarely seen.

The feathers merge with their surroundings, and the birds stretch their head and neck upward to mimic the reeds. Should the reeds sway in a strong wind, the bird will also sway to maintain the camouflage.

The parents make the nest among the swamp vegetation, bending reeds to create a suitable platform, but the nest may also be built above the waterline on a tree limb. Usually four eggs are laid, in the spring or early summer.

Dusky Moorhen

Moorhen is an Old English name, originally 'mere hen', a creature of meres or freshwater lakes. In the wild, moorhens skulk among the plant life and are rarely seen, but birds living in ornamental lakes soon learn that people are harmless and become tame.

Moorhens eat water plants in quantity and also graze on land. In the early morning they can be seen well away from lake edges, but if danger threatens they quickly return to the water.

They build a nest of weeds, raised above water level, and lay up to ten eggs, sometimes even more. The pair defends the territory around the nest, driving off intruders. On hatching, the baby is a fascinating ball of jet black down, with a touch of bright red on the beak. It becomes lankier; an immature moorhen resembles its parents, but has brown plumage and a greenish-yellow beak, rather than the red one of the adult.

Woodhen

The woodhen lives only on Lord Howe Island. Many flightless island species became extinct after the arrival of humans and this almost happened to the woodhen. First it was hunted as food, to make woodhen pies, and later killed as a pest because it stole eggs from the fowlyards of early settlers. Added to this, pigs became wild and ate both eggs and chicks.

By 1969, fewer than twenty birds were left and extinction seemed certain. Pressure from conservationists forced the eradication of the pigs and, later, a breeding in captivity programme was funded by the New South Wales National Parks and Wildlife Foundation. This was a great success.

The photograph shows three young birds in their breeding enclosure just before their release into the wild. Today, several years and $300 000 later, woodhens can be seen in most parts of the island, a heartwarming conservation success story.

Banded Plover (Banded Lapwing)

A screaming fury hurtling from the sky is the first warning a human intruder has that a plover's nest or chicks is near. If direct attack fails, either of the parents may pretend to have a broken wing, or at least imitate a bird unable to fly, to tempt a hunter away from the eggs or chicks.

The nests are usually built in a small hollow on the ground, and the four eggs neatly tucked together look almost like the soil on which they are lying, so few enemies see them. The chicks are equally well camouflaged and the parents soon move away from the nest site with their family. The youngsters 'freeze' when the parents give a warning call. Since it is movement that normally reveals the presence of an animal, this technique usually succeeds in safeguarding the chicks.

Banded plovers nest in the drier grasslands of Australia but at times will nest in the heart of a city, even on a factory roof. *(Photograph Bob Miller)*

White-breasted Sea-eagle

Sea-eagles are found around the world and the American bald eagle, the emblem of the United States, belongs to this group. Our sea-eagle is the second largest bird of prey in Australia, only the wedge-tailed eagle being larger.

They live all around the Australian coastline and inland along the larger rivers, but can also be seen almost in the heart of cities if there is enough bushland for a pair to nest. The adults eat a variety of animals, feeding both in the water and on the land, as well as scavenging along beaches.

They build giant nests of sticks high in trees and on a treeless island will create a tall structure on the ground. The female lays two eggs and carries out the bulk of the incubation, the male at times giving a little help. The young bird in the photograph, born in a nest in a mangrove tree, had left its high spot to wander around the lagoon in the mangrove forest while waiting for its parents to return with food.

Wedge-tailed Eagle

The wedge-tailed eagle is the largest Australian bird of prey, and may be the fourth largest of world eagles.

The parents place a nesting platform of sticks high in a tree, lining it with green leaves. These are renewed regularly when the young are in the nest, perhaps because they help keep the platform cool.

Two eggs are the usual clutch. Both parents incubate the eggs, and then provide the chicks with a variety of food, ranging from rabbits to lizards.

Until recently farmers regarded these eagles as pests, believing they killed lambs, but research has shown these magnificent birds are of little importance to the sheep industry. Most of the lambs eaten are either dead or dying, and it is very rare for an eagle to kill a healthy one. Indeed the birds are useful as they eat rabbits, a serious pest for farmers. *(Photograph Bob Miller)*

Malleefowl

Instead of sitting on the eggs and keeping the clutch warm by heat from their bodies, the Australian mound builders create incubators with a mound of earth and leaves to keep the eggs at a constant temperature so the chicks will develop normally.

The brush-turkey and the scrubfowl live in the warm, wet forests of the mainland. The malleefowl, living in arid country in southern Australia, faces more problems than the birds of the pleasantly warm and humid tropical forests.

Nesting for the malleefowl takes place from early spring through to autumn. During this time the ground temperature can rise from freezing point to over 40 °C, yet the male, doing the bulk of the work, keeps the egg temperatures around 33 °C for almost eight months.

During the early stages of nesting the break-down of leaf material may create too much heat, so the malleefowl goes to the mound in the cool of the early morning and scrapes away the surface, leaving only a thin layer of soil over the eggs so the heat can escape. Later the bird scrapes back the sand to keep the eggs warm through the chill of night. It seems to be able to predict heavy rain and heaps the mound even higher before a downfall.

In late summer when there is little leaf material left, the male opens the mound in late morning and allows the sun to warm the eggs; in the late afternoon he scrapes warm sand back again. The male is able to test the temperature of the mound by scraping away some of the surface soil and sampling a mouthful; either the mouth lining or the tongue serves as a thermometer.

The chick hatches perhaps 50 centimetres or more below the surface and pushes its way up at a rate of about 30 centimetres an hour. By the time it reaches the surface its feathers are dry and fluffy. It is an exciting moment to see the chick push its head above ground, take a quick look about to see if danger threatens, and then climb out and run off briskly into the nearby bush. If threatened it can fly off.

The photograph shows the malleefowl on the open mound.

Painted Quail

Animals that live on the ground avoid danger by a variety of techniques. Quail can run swiftly, or when approached, fly rapidly upward.

In an unusual reversal of the normal in birds, the female is larger and has brighter plumage than the male. In keeping with this difference the female mates with a number of males during the breeding season, and the males do most of the nest building as well as care for the four eggs and the young.

The chicks are beautifully camouflaged, and so are well protected. *(Photograph Bob Miller)*

Torresian Imperial Pigeon (Torres Strait Pigeon or Nutmeg Pigeon)

The Torresian pigeon ranges over much of northern Australia and south along the eastern coast to the Tropic of Capricorn, so perhaps a more fitting name is nutmeg pigeon. In Australia the birds appear to eat a variety of fruits of the rainforest trees of the mainland coastal forests, although not many nutmegs.

The pigeons are migratory, leaving New Guinea for Australia in winter and establishing nesting territories on offshore islands. At times huge numbers will occupy an island although the adults must travel to the nearby mainland for food for themselves, and later for the young. The sound of the loud cooing of thousands of pigeons becomes almost deafening on some islands.

The nest is the typical rickety one produced by all members of this group. Often the egg or chick can be seen from below through gaps in the twigs. Only one egg is laid and the parents take turns in incubating it. Three to four weeks later the naked chick is born.

All pigeons are unique in that the crop produces a substance called pigeon's milk, rich in protein, fat and vitamins. This is a complete food and is regurgitated to the newly hatched chick. Later the milk is mixed with wild fruit, but when it is ready to fly the youngster is fed entirely on the fruits.

Orange-bellied Parrot *(Right)*

Australia was once called the Land of Parrots, in a tribute to the variety and beauty of our local species. The orange-bellied parrot is probably the rarest of the group, and unless it is given careful conservation management, it might become extinct.

It breeds only in Tasmania and not many nests have been found, but all were in hollows in trees, usually old, gnarled eucalypts. Egg-laying is towards the end of November and the mother incubates up to six eggs, although the male visits and feeds her regularly, often every few hours.

When the babies hatch both parents feed them, often travelling up to 5 kilometres searching for the seeds of coastal grasses and other plants.

In March the birds leave their breeding place in south-west Tasmania for winter feeding in Victoria and South Australia. *(Photograph Dave Watts)*

Swift Parrot

Everyone is able to recognise a parrot. All the family have the typical beak—the upper and lower parts both move—making it ideal for crushing nuts and other hard food items. All have two toes pointing forward and two backward, making the foot excellent for grasping things. The tongue is not only thick but prehensile; sometimes in the nectar feeders it has a brush-like appendage.

Parrots, parakeets, lorikeets and cockatoos are all members of the family but generally cockatoos are large and square-tailed while parrots have long, slim, rounded tails.

Most parrots nest in a hollow of some kind so there is no need for camouflage colours for the eggs. It is more important for them to be easily seen in the darkness, so they are white.

In Tasmania and nearby islands the swift parrots move in noisy groups through flowering trees, feeding on nectar, pollen and also insects, then taking off with their characteristic rapid flight.

Up to five round eggs are incubated by the mother for about three weeks in nests in hollow trees and some two months later the young leave the nest. *(Photograph Dave Watts)*

Cuckoo

Cuckoos have an evil reputation because of their habit of laying eggs in the nests of other birds and leaving the onerous child-care duties to foster parents. Australia has eleven kinds of cuckoo, from the sparrow-sized bronze-cuckoos to the channel-billed cuckoo that attains the bulk of a magpie.

Cuckoos generally choose foster parents that are insect eaters, avoiding seed-eating birds. Each species shows a preference for a selected range of 'victims' and often their eggs are similar. The mother cuckoo may keep a close watch on the other bird's nest-building and if egg-laying is well advanced she will take out the rightful eggs and substitute her own. She may even destroy the nest so the foster parent has to start again.

When the cuckoo hatches, blind and naked, it moves restlessly, burrowing under other eggs or chicks, until it gets them on to the small of its back. Then it moves to the nest edge, grips tightly and heaves the load over the brink. The baby cuckoo continues this culling until all the nest mates or eggs are discarded. If a kind-hearted person replaces the rightful babies they will be tossed out again.

Sometimes the cuckoo chick is so huge the foster parents, despite working from daylight to dark, may not be able to satisfy its gargantuan appetite. Young cuckoos have an appealing food-begging call and posture, and a queue of foster parents will often form, all fighting for the privilege of feeding it.

The photograph shows a young pallid cuckoo with a grey fantail. The pallid cuckoo had been fostered by a fuscous honeyeater but moved over to the grey fantail's nest with young in it. The grey fantail's babies died of neglect while the pallid cuckoo, now even larger than its foster parent, flourished. *(Photograph Norman Chaffer)*

White-naped Honeyeater

Half of the world's birds belong to a group called the perching birds. Most spend their lives in shrubs or trees, with the foot ideal for gripping a branch, hence the name.

All the chicks in this large group are born blind, naked and almost helpless, except for an ability to devour food! It is usual for both parents to care for the eggs and young, as can be seen in this photograph.

Honeyeaters are a group of Australian birds that feed on nectar and pollen, but also eat insects that visit bush flowers. The white-naped honeyeaters shown here obtain about three-quarters of their food by searching the leaves of trees for insects and spiders, with the blossoms as a bonus. *(Photograph Bob Miller)*

Red-capped Robin

The male red-capped robin photographed here is staring at its own egg, rising as if by magic from the bottom of the deep nest.

A female bronze cuckoo had laid an egg among the robin's eggs and the baby cuckoo hatched first. The first day of its life the cuckoo chick squirmed around until it had a robin egg resting in the small of its back. Then the youngster moved upward until it reached the rim of the nest. It shrugged the egg up and out of the nest. A few hours later it had managed to throw out the second egg.

Crimson Chat

Crimson chats, colourful birds of the drier regions of mainland Australia, build their nest in a shrub close to the ground. Usually three eggs are laid. The male, shown here, is much brighter than the female.

Both share in nesting duties and, like the honeyeaters, the adults have brushtipped tongues, suitable for gathering nectar and pollen. Flowering in the dry country is spasmodic, so the birds feed mainly on insects.

The chats are probably the great nomads of Australian birds, travelling many kilometres in search of food. *(Photograph Bob Miller)*